D1356213

ATLAS OF MINIATURE ADVENTURES

WIDE EYED EDITIONS

CONTENTS

THE WORLD IS FULL OF MINI MARVELS...

Big things get a lot of attention: the planet's longest rivers, tallest mountains, and highest buildings are tourist hotspots, featured in record books the world over. But what about the small things?

This book celebrates life's little wonders, from the world's tiniest animals to its miniature works of art, intricate model villages, pint-sized plants, teeny toys, and even its smallest countries. These mini marvels show that the best – and the quirkiest – things really do come in small packages.

EUROPE

From model villages and mini museums to the world's smallest country, Europe is packed full of wee wonders waiting to be discovered.

Iceland

Faroe Islands

Shetland Islands

Strum along with the UKULELE ORCHESTRA OF GREAT BRITAIN (UK)

Ride in the Peel P50, the SMALLEST CAR IN THE WORLD (Isle of Man, UK)

See Holland in miniature at MADURODAM (Netherlands)

Ireland

United Kingdom

Netherlands

Take a trip back in time at BEKONSCOT MODEL VILLAGE (UK)

Explore a continent in miniature at MINI-EUROPE (Belgium)

Belgium   Luxembe

North Atlantic Ocean

Play the giant at the MUSÉE MINIATURE (France)

Switzerland

Liechtenstein

Think outside the box at the MATCHBOX MUSEUM (Portugal)

France

It

Monaco

Sar
Ma

Portugal

Spain

Mediterranean Sea

Corsica

Balearic Islands

Sardini

White Sea

Baltic Sea

eden

Finland

Russia

Gotland

Estonia

Latvia

Lithuania

Kaliningrad Oblast

Belarus

Tee off in the dark at
BLACK LIGHT MINIGOLF
(Germany)

zech
epublic

Poland

Shake things up at the
PERZY SNOW
GLOBE MUSEUM
(Austria)

Ukraine

Slovakia

Moldova

Marvel at the
MUSEUM OF
MICRO-ART
(Hungary)

Hungary

Romania

a

Croatia

Serbia

Black
Sea

Asia

Bosnia &
Herzegovina

Montenegro

Kosovo

Macedonia

Bulgaria

Albania

Turkey

isit the SMALLEST
NTRY IN THE WORLD
(Vatican City)

Greece

Turkey

Discover Miniatürk,
the world's LARGEST
MINIATURE PARK (Turkey)

cily

ta

Cyprus

9

Bekonscot has welcomed over 14 million visitors since 1929, including the Queen, who used to visit on her birthday as a child.

BUCKINGHAMSHIRE, UK

The railway that runs through Bekonscot is one of the largest model railways in the UK.

10

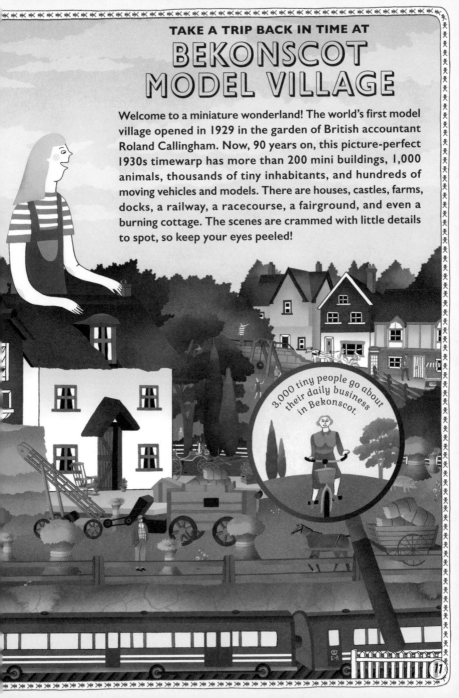

TAKE A TRIP BACK IN TIME AT
BEKONSCOT
MODEL VILLAGE

Welcome to a miniature wonderland! The world's first model village opened in 1929 in the garden of British accountant Roland Callingham. Now, 90 years on, this picture-perfect 1930s timewarp has more than 200 mini buildings, 1,000 animals, thousands of tiny inhabitants, and hundreds of moving vehicles and models. There are houses, castles, farms, docks, a railway, a racecourse, a fairground, and even a burning cottage. The scenes are crammed with little details to spot, so keep your eyes peeled!

3,000 tiny people go about their daily business in Bekonscot.

In 1952, the teenage Princess Beatrix was appointed mayor of Madurodam. Now, a new mayor is elected every year from a 'city council' of local schoolchildren.

THE HAGUE · THE NETHERLANDS

Madurodam's mini residents change with the seasons: in summer they wear T-shirts, and in winter they wrap up warm.

12

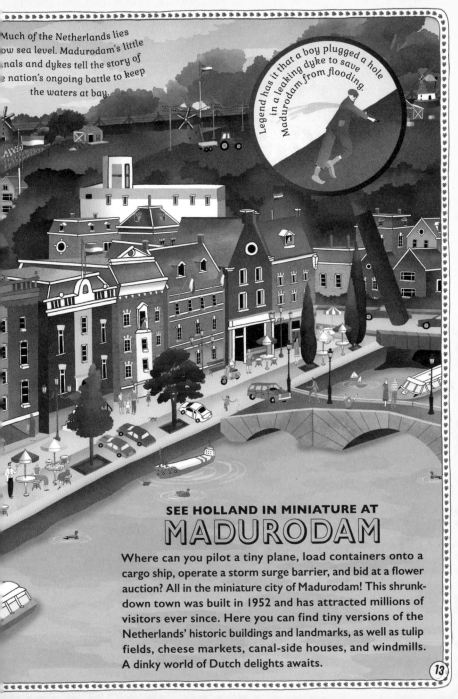

Much of the Netherlands lies below sea level. Madurodam's little canals and dykes tell the story of the nation's ongoing battle to keep the waters at bay.

Legend has it that a boy plugged a hole in a leaking dyke to save Madurodam from flooding.

SEE HOLLAND IN MINIATURE AT
MADURODAM

Where can you pilot a tiny plane, load containers onto a cargo ship, operate a storm surge barrier, and bid at a flower auction? All in the miniature city of Madurodam! This shrunk-down town was built in 1952 and has attracted millions of visitors ever since. Here you can find tiny versions of the Netherlands' historic buildings and landmarks, as well as tulip fields, cheese markets, canal-side houses, and windmills. A dinky world of Dutch delights awaits.

TEE OFF IN THE DARK AT
BLACK LIGHT MINIGOLF

This is minigolf as you've never seen it before. Tucked away beneath Berlin's Görlitzer Park, in the cellar of an old train station, are 18 holes of miniature glow-in-the-dark fun. In this crazily-coloured neon world you can hit your golf ball past famous Berlin landmarks, through strange undersea scenes, and into futuristic space-age landscapes. Get putting!

BERLIN, GERMANY

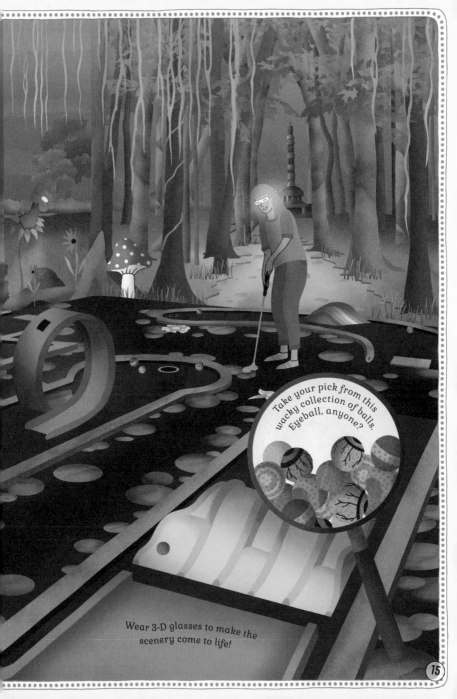

Take your pick from this wacky collection of balls. Eyeball, anyone?

Wear 3-D glasses to make the scenery come to life!

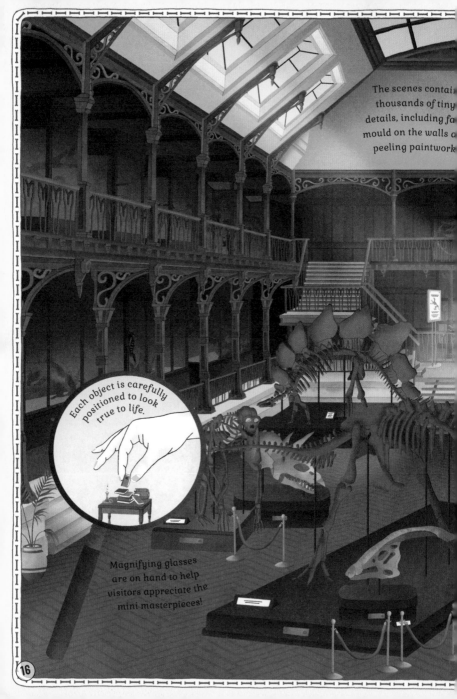

The scenes contain thousands of tiny details, including fake mould on the walls and peeling paintwork.

Each object is carefully positioned to look true to life.

Magnifying glasses are on hand to help visitors appreciate the mini masterpieces!

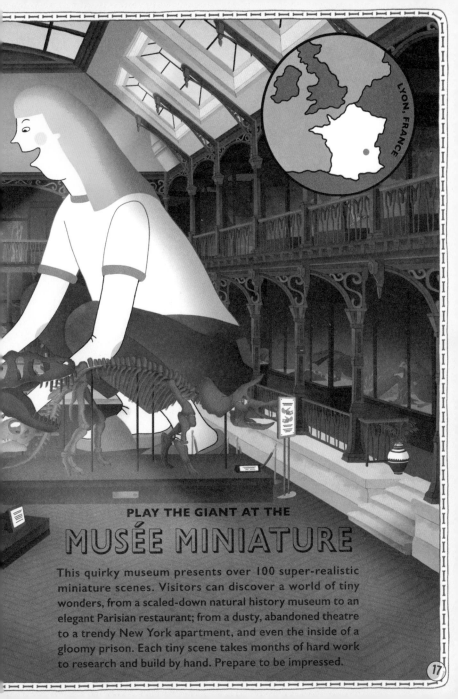

LYON, FRANCE

PLAY THE GIANT AT THE

MUSÉE MINIATURE

This quirky museum presents over 100 super-realistic miniature scenes. Visitors can discover a world of tiny wonders, from a scaled-down natural history museum to an elegant Parisian restaurant; from a dusty, abandoned theatre to a trendy New York apartment, and even the inside of a gloomy prison. Each tiny scene takes months of hard work to research and build by hand. Prepare to be impressed.

17

SHAKE THINGS UP AT THE
PERZY SNOW GLOBE MUSEUM

Snow globes were invented in 1900 by an Austrian named Erwin Perzy, who made surgical instruments. He was trying to increase the brightness of a lightbulb by placing a glass globe in front of it, filled with water. He experimented by adding grains of white powder to the water to reflect the light, and the snow globe was born! Today, visitors to this Vienna museum can learn about the history of these miniature winter wonderlands in the place where it all began.

The recipe for the fake snow is a closely guarded secret!

VIENNA, AUSTRIA

Erwin Perzy's grandson now runs the company, which produces about 200,000 snow globes a year.

Perzy's first snow globe contained a tiny model of Austria's Maria Zell Basilica.

The museum has a replica of a snow globe made for U.S. president Bill Clinton, containing real confetti from his inauguration.

AFRICA

Safari-lovers will have heard of Africa's 'Big Five' animals, but this vast continent is also home to some incredible tiny creatures, as well as some very ancient miniature monuments.

Madeira

Canary Islands

Morocco

Western Sahara

Mauritania

Mali

North Atlantic Ocean

Cape Verde

Senegal

The Gambia

Guinea-Bissau

Guinea

Burkina

Sierra Leone

Ivory Coast

Liberia

Wallow with the
PYGMY HIPPOS
(Liberia)

Bow to the tiny
ROYAL ANTELOPE
(Ghana)

Ascension Island

Plod along with the
SMALLEST TORTOISE
IN THE WORLD
(Namibia)

St Helena

South Atlantic Ocean

Stop off at the
OUTENIQUA MOON
RAILWAY
(South Africa)

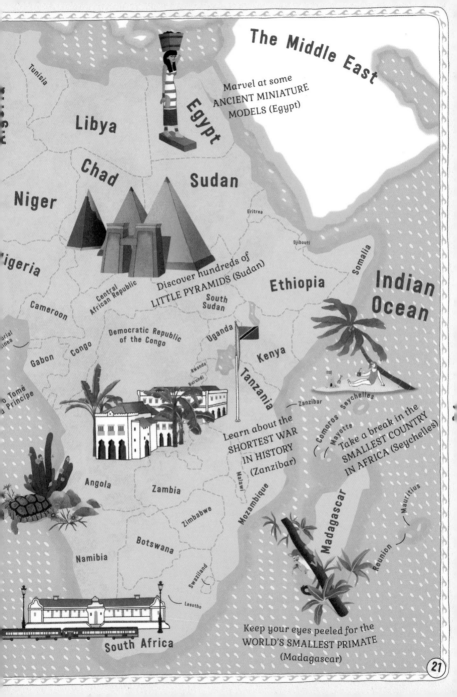

Tunisia

Libya

Egypt

Marvel at some
ANCIENT MINIATURE
MODELS (Egypt)

Chad

Sudan

Niger

Eritrea

Djibouti

igeria

Nigeria

Central
African Republic

Discover hundreds of
LITTLE PYRAMIDS (Sudan)

South
Sudan

Ethiopia

Somalia

Indian
Ocean

Cameroon

Democratic Republic
of the Congo

Uganda

Kenya

torial
inea

Gabon

Congo

Rwanda

Burundi

Tanzania

o Tomé
u Príncipe

Zanzibar

Comoros

Seychelles

Mayotte

Learn about the
SHORTEST WAR
IN HISTORY
(Zanzibar)

Take a break in the
SMALLEST COUNTRY
IN AFRICA (Seychelles)

Angola

Zambia

Malawi

Mozambique

Madagascar

Mauritius

Zimbabwe

Réunion

Botswana

Namibia

Swaziland

Lesotho

South Africa

Keep your eyes peeled for the
WORLD'S SMALLEST PRIMATE
(Madagascar)

21

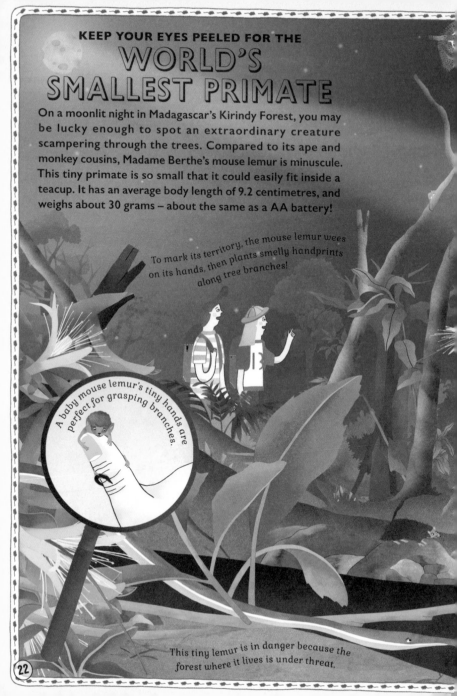

KEEP YOUR EYES PEELED FOR THE
WORLD'S SMALLEST PRIMATE

On a moonlit night in Madagascar's Kirindy Forest, you may be lucky enough to spot an extraordinary creature scampering through the trees. Compared to its ape and monkey cousins, Madame Berthe's mouse lemur is minuscule. This tiny primate is so small that it could easily fit inside a teacup. It has an average body length of 9.2 centimetres, and weighs about 30 grams – about the same as a AA battery!

To mark its territory, the mouse lemur wees on its hands, then plants smelly handprints along tree branches!

A baby mouse lemur's tiny hands are perfect for grasping branches.

This tiny lemur is in danger because the forest where it lives is under threat.

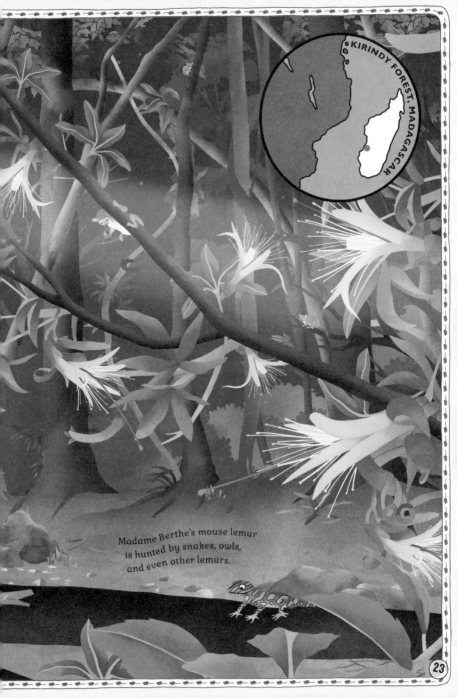

KIRINDY FOREST, MADAGASCAR

Madame Berthe's mouse lemur
is hunted by snakes, owls,
and even other lemurs.

NAMIBIA & SOUTH AFRICA

This little tortoise spends most of the summer and winter hiding away, but it comes out in spring to feed on juicy plants.

PLOD ALONG WITH THE
SMALLEST TORTOISE IN THE WORLD

Living on the rocky hillsides of South Africa and Namibia is a teeny, tiny tortoise. The speckled padloper is a hardy survivor, sheltering from blistering summer sun or freezing winter temperatures in rocky crevices. Thought to be the smallest tortoise in the world, the male speckled padloper is titchy enough to hold in the palm of your hand!

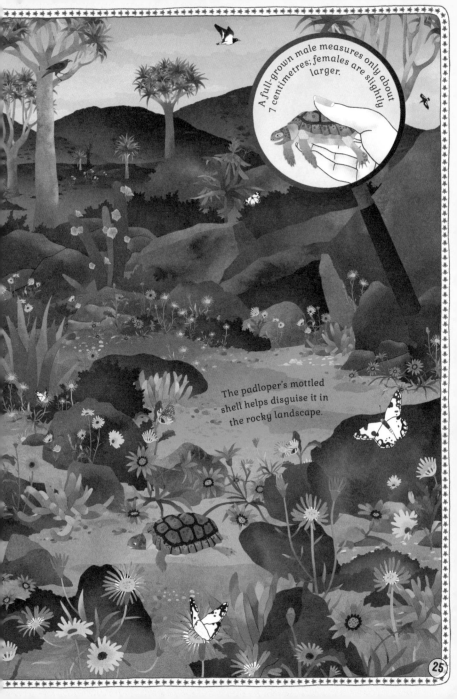

A full-grown male measures only about 7 centimetres; females are slightly larger.

The padloper's mottled shell helps disguise it in the rocky landscape.

Arctic Ocean

Greenland

Davis Strait

Alaska
(USA)

Go sandboarding
in the SMALLEST
DESERT IN THE
WORLD (Canada)

Gulf of Alaska

Hudson
Bay

Canada

Get burrowing
with the
PYGMY RABBIT
(USA)

Send a letter with the
WORLD'S SMALLEST
POSTAL SERVICE (USA)

Visit small-town
America at the
ROADSIDE AMERICA
MODEL VILLAGE (USA)

United States
of America

Take a peek at one of the
WORLD'S SMALLEST
BUTTERFLIES (USA)

Mexico

Take a little bite
of a tiny
MEXICAN CUCUMBER
(Mexico)

Gulf of Mexico

North
Pacific
Ocean

NORTH AMERICA

North America's little landmarks are big in personality, from one of the world's largest model railways to the planet's most lavish doll's house – and don't forget those mini presidents!

Discover one of the WORLD'S SMALLEST DINOSAUR FOOTPRINTS (Canada)

Discover one of the WORLD'S LARGEST MODEL RAILWAYS (USA)

North Atlantic Ocean

Azores

Bermuda

rgasso Sea

et the AMERICAN PRESIDENTS IN MINIATURE at the residents Hall of Fame (USA)

Caribbean Sea

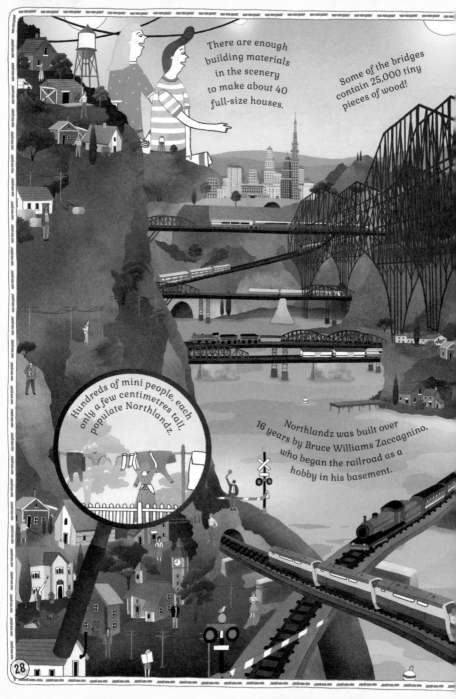

There are enough building materials in the scenery to make about 40 full-size houses.

Some of the bridges contain 25,000 tiny pieces of wood!

Hundreds of mini people, each only a few centimetres tall, populate Northlandz.

Northlandz was built over 16 years by Bruce Williams Zaccagnino, who began the railroad as a hobby in his basement.

NEW JERSEY, USA

DISCOVER ONE OF THE WORLD'S LARGEST
MODEL RAILWAYS

With over 100 trains, 12 kilometres of track, 3,000 buildings, and half a million little trees, Northlandz Model Railroad in Flemington, New Jersey, is one of the largest model railways in the world. In this vast miniature world, tiny trains emerge from dark tunnels, speeding along rocky cliff-sides and across steep canyons, past pocket-sized people, teeny towns, and small-scale skyscrapers. All aboard for an adventure!

FALL UNDER A SPELL AT THE
FAIRY CASTLE

At Chicago's Museum of Science and Industry you will discover the most lavish doll's house in the world. Measuring 2.4 metres tall, with diamond-encrusted chandeliers, tiny gold cutlery, marble floors, and miniature works of art, the Fairy Castle is a palace fit for a pocket-sized princess. Created in the 1930s by silent film star Colleen Moore, the castle took seven years to complete and cost half a million dollars – which is equal to about seven million dollars today!

In the prince's bedroom there's a 'bearskin' rug made from ermine fur and mouse teeth!

The drawing room has a painting of Mickey and Minnie Mouse donated by Walt Disney.

Some tiny glass slippers are on display, measuring just 6 millimetres!

Over 100 architects, designers, and artists from around the world worked on the Fairy Castle.

CHICAGO, USA

In the bathroom, the bath is made of silver and real water can flow from the dolphins' mouths!

The tapestries in the dining room have stitches so small they can only be seen under a microscope.

TAKE A PEEK AT ONE OF THE
WORLD'S SMALLEST BUTTERFLIES

On the salt marshes of the south-western United States, keen-eyed nature lovers may spy one of the tiniest butterflies on the planet. The western pygmy blue has a wingspan of only 1.2 centimetres – it's the size of a fingernail! This little gem flutters close to the ground, so it's easy to miss unless you look very carefully.

Blink and you'll miss it!

The pygmy blue butterfly slurps up nectar from flowers using a long feeding tube.

SOUTH-WEST USA

Pygmy blue caterpillars have a useful relationship with ants. They produce a sweet liquid for the ants to eat and, in return, the ants protect them from predators.

SEND A LETTER WITH THE
WORLD'S SMALLEST POST SERVICE

When artist Lea Redmond was waking up from a nap one day, the idea of a teeny tiny letter popped into her head. She is now postmaster of the World's Smallest Post Service: a San Francisco-based business that makes itty bitty letters for people to send to their loved ones all around the world. As well as letters, they make tiny greetings cards, invitations and gifts, and have even sent a few miniature marriage proposals!

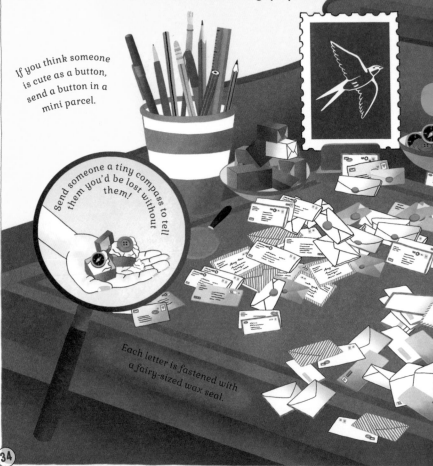

If you think someone is cute as a button, send a button in a mini parcel.

Send someone a tiny compass to tell them you'd be lost without them!

Each letter is fastened with a fairy-sized wax seal.

Before the letters are posted, they are sealed inside a larger envelope so they don't get lost in the mail.

SAN FRANCISCO, USA

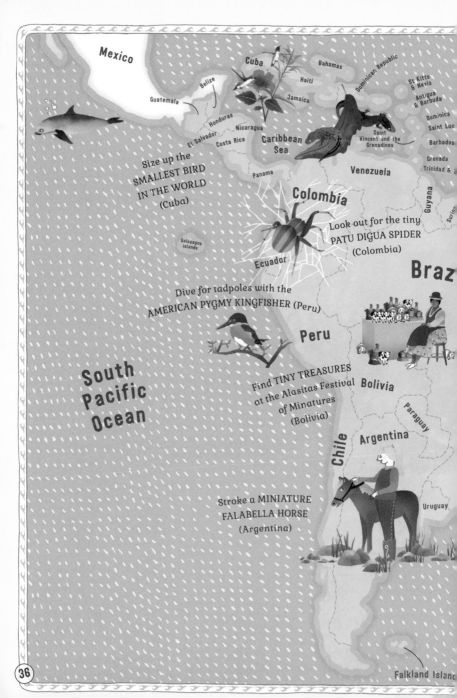

Mexico

Cuba

Bahamas

Haiti

Dominican Republic

Belize

Guatemala

Jamaica

St Kitts & Nevis

Antigua & Barbuda

Dominica

Honduras

El Salvador
Nicaragua

Saint Luc

Costa Rica

Caribbean
Sea

Saint
Vincent and the
Grenadines

Barbados

Size up the
SMALLEST BIRD
IN THE WORLD
(Cuba)

Panama

Venezuela

Grenada

Trinidad &

Colombia

Guyana

Surin

Look out for the tiny
PATU DIGUA SPIDER
(Colombia)

Galápagos
Islands

Ecuador

Braz

Dive for tadpoles with the
AMERICAN PYGMY KINGFISHER (Peru)

Peru

South
Pacific
Ocean

Find TINY TREASURES
at the Alasitas Festival
of Minatures
(Bolivia)

Bolivia

Paraguay

Chile

Argentina

Stroke a MINIATURE
FALABELLA HORSE
(Argentina)

Uruguay

36

Falkland Island

CENTRAL & SOUTH AMERICA

This continent is famous for amazing wildlife, so it's no surprise that here you'll find some of the tiniest creatures on the planet.

away with one of the
TTLEST LIZARDS
N THE WORLD
(inican Republic)

Meet the world's smallest monkey, the PYGMY MARMOSET (Brazil)

South
Atlantic
Ocean

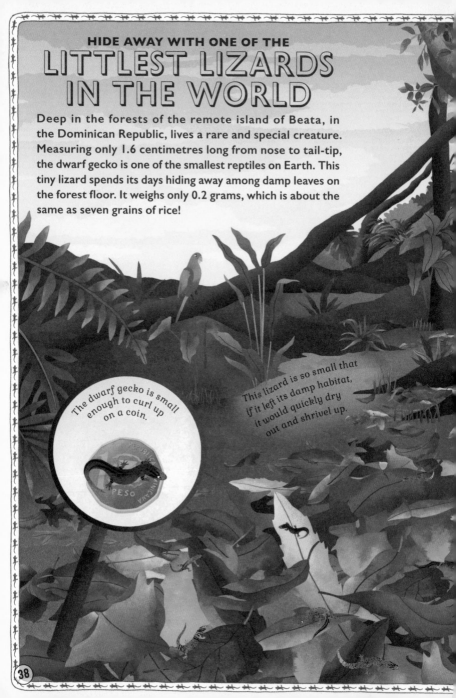

HIDE AWAY WITH ONE OF THE
LITTLEST LIZARDS IN THE WORLD

Deep in the forests of the remote island of Beata, in the Dominican Republic, lives a rare and special creature. Measuring only 1.6 centimetres long from nose to tail-tip, the dwarf gecko is one of the smallest reptiles on Earth. This tiny lizard spends its days hiding away among damp leaves on the forest floor. It weighs only 0.2 grams, which is about the same as seven grains of rice!

The dwarf gecko is small enough to curl up on a coin.

This lizard is so small that if it left its damp habitat, it would quickly dry out and shrivel up.

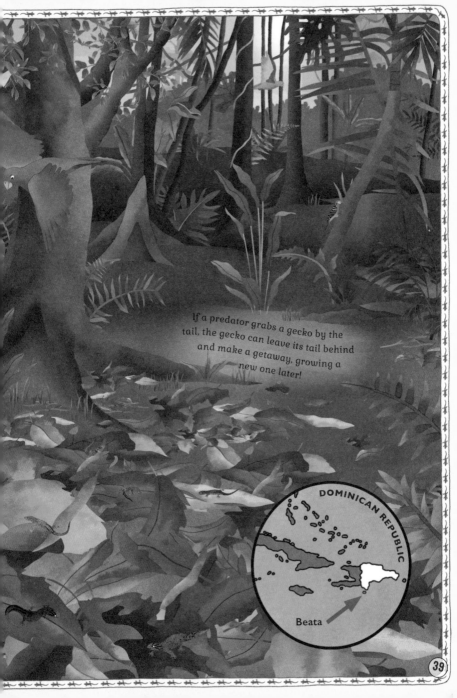

If a predator grabs a gecko by the tail, the gecko can leave its tail behind and make a getaway, growing a new one later!

DOMINICAN REPUBLIC

Beata

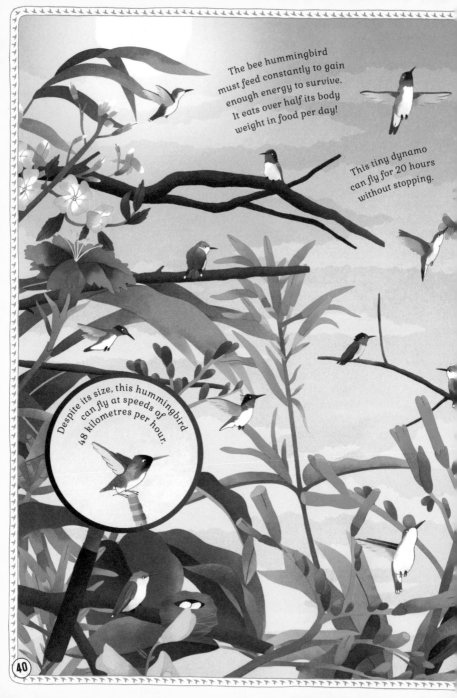

The bee hummingbird must feed constantly to gain enough energy to survive. It eats over half its body weight in food per day!

This tiny dynamo can fly for 20 hours without stopping.

Despite its size, this hummingbird can fly at speeds of 48 kilometres per hour.

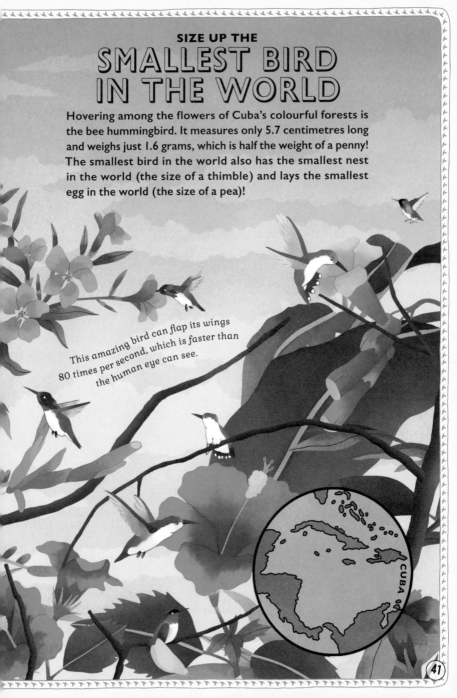

SIZE UP THE
SMALLEST BIRD IN THE WORLD

Hovering among the flowers of Cuba's colourful forests is the bee hummingbird. It measures only 5.7 centimetres long and weighs just 1.6 grams, which is half the weight of a penny! The smallest bird in the world also has the smallest nest in the world (the size of a thimble) and lays the smallest egg in the world (the size of a pea)!

This amazing bird can flap its wings 80 times per second, which is faster than the human eye can see.

CUBA

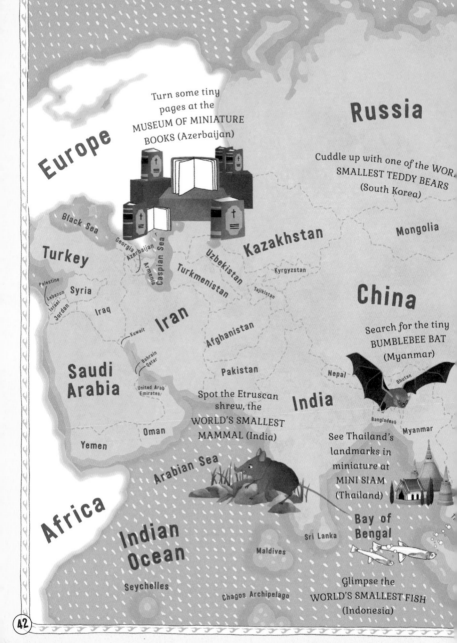

Turn some tiny pages at the MUSEUM OF MINIATURE BOOKS (Azerbaijan)

Russia

Cuddle up with one of the WORL... SMALLEST TEDDY BEARS (South Korea)

Europe

Black Sea

Turkey

Palestine
Lebanon
Israel
Syria
Jordan
Iraq

Georgia
Azerbaijan
Armenia
Caspian Sea

Kazakhstan

Uzbekistan

Turkmenistan

Kyrgyzstan

Tajikistan

Mongolia

China

Kuwait

Iran

Afghanistan

Nepal

Bhutan

Search for the tiny BUMBLEBEE BAT (Myanmar)

Saudi Arabia

Bahrain
Qatar

United Arab Emirates

Pakistan

India

Bangladesh

Myanmar

Oman

Spot the Etruscan shrew, the WORLD'S SMALLEST MAMMAL (India)

Yemen

See Thailand's landmarks in miniature at MINI SIAM (Thailand)

Arabian Sea

Bay of Bengal

Africa

Indian Ocean

Sri Lanka

Maldives

Seychelles

Chagos Archipelago

Glimpse the WORLD'S SMALLEST FISH (Indonesia)

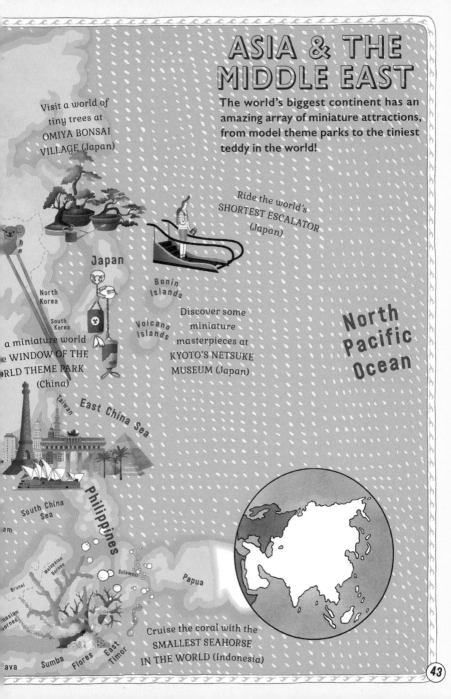

ASIA & THE MIDDLE EAST

The world's biggest continent has an amazing array of miniature attractions, from model theme parks to the tiniest teddy in the world!

Visit a world of tiny trees at OMIYA BONSAI VILLAGE (Japan)

Ride the world's SHORTEST ESCALATOR (Japan)

Discover some miniature masterpieces at KYOTO'S NETSUKE MUSEUM (Japan)

a miniature world e WINDOW OF THE RLD THEME PARK (China)

Cruise the coral with the SMALLEST SEAHORSE IN THE WORLD (Indonesia)

Japan

North Korea

South Korea

Bonin Islands

Volcano Islands

North Pacific Ocean

Taiwan

East China Sea

South China Sea

Philippines

am

Malaysian Borneo

Brunei

nesian orneo

Sulawesi

Papua

ava

Sumba

Flores

East Timor

The bonsai village contains thousands of miniature trees. There are several different bonsai nurseries and a museum.

Styles of Bonsai Tree

Formal upright
Informal upright
Slanting
Windswept
Cascade
Forest

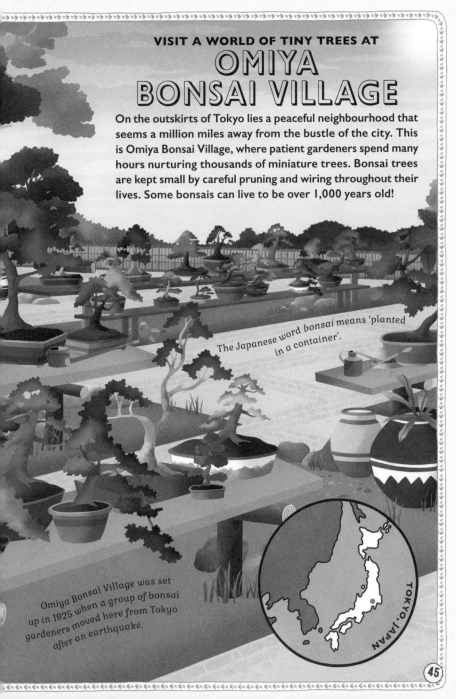

VISIT A WORLD OF TINY TREES AT
OMIYA BONSAI VILLAGE

On the outskirts of Tokyo lies a peaceful neighbourhood that seems a million miles away from the bustle of the city. This is Omiya Bonsai Village, where patient gardeners spend many hours nurturing thousands of miniature trees. Bonsai trees are kept small by careful pruning and wiring throughout their lives. Some bonsais can live to be over 1,000 years old!

The Japanese word bonsai means 'planted in a container'.

Omiya Bonsai Village was set up in 1925 when a group of bonsai gardeners moved here from Tokyo after an earthquake.

TOKYO, JAPAN

KYOTO, JAPAN

The Netsuke Museum is housed in a building constructed for samurai (Japanese warriors) in 1820.

Netsuke depict people, animals, mythical creatures and more.

DISCOVER SOME MINIATURE MASTERPIECES AT

KYOTO'S NETSUKE MUSEUM

Hundreds of years ago in Japan, men wore small toggles called *netsuke* as fasteners on their clothing. These objects were made out of ivory, wood, or porcelain, and were often very intricately carved. Today, the Netsuke Museum in Kyoto showcases hundreds of these miniature works of art, with plenty of magnifying glasses on hand so visitors can appreciate their finer details!

Traditional Japanese clothes had no pockets, so men carried things in pouches. A netsuke was used to fasten a pouch to a belt. It quickly became a hot fashion accessory!

JEJU ISLAND, SOUTH KOREA

This museum also boasts a Mona Lisa teddy, an Elvis teddy and an army of terracotta teddy warriors.

Also on display is one of the world's most expensive bears, created by Louis Vuitton and Steiff. It sold in 2000 for $2.1 million!

Tiny Ted was made in 2006 by South African bear artist Cheryl Moss.

CUDDLE UP WITH ONE OF THE
WORLD'S SMALLEST TEDDY BEARS

If you want to meet one of the smallest teddy bears on the planet, head to the Teddy Bear Museum on Jeju Island, South Korea. The size of a pea, Tiny Ted is only 4.5 millimetres high. This miniature marvel was stitched in exactly the same way as a larger teddy, so he has jointed arms and legs and a head that can swivel. Don't breathe too deeply when you're close to him, as you might inhale him!

SMALLEST SEAHORSE IN THE WORLD

Satomi's pygmy seahorse is possibly the tiniest seahorse on Earth, measuring a weeny 14 millimetres in length, which is smaller than a penny. This minuscule fish lives among the coral reefs off Indonesia's Derawan Islands. It wasn't discovered until 2008, partly because it is so tiny, and partly because it is nocturnal, hiding away during the day. Eagle-eyed divers, take note!

Satomi's seahorse is the smallest seahorse found so far, but there might be tinier species out there...

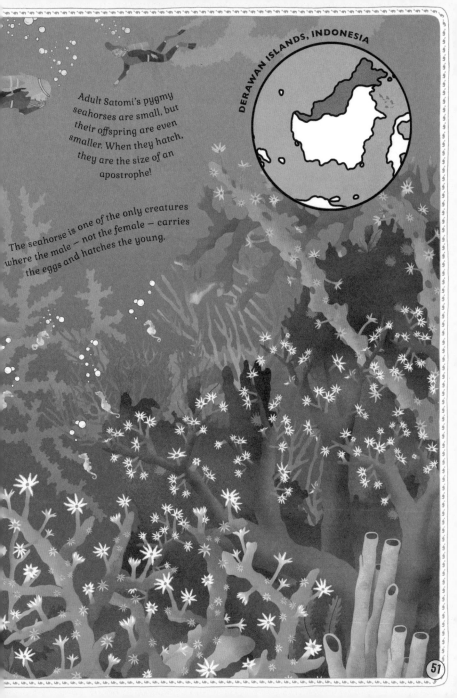

Adult Satomi's pygmy seahorses are small, but their offspring are even smaller. When they hatch, they are the size of an apostrophe!

The seahorse is one of the only creatures where the male – not the female – carries the eggs and hatches the young.

DERAWAN ISLANDS, INDONESIA

AUSTRALASIA & OCEANIA

From tiny desert fish to hidden garden gnomes and little hobbit houses, Australasia has its fair share of quirky mini marvels.

Seek out the WORLD'S SMALLEST FROG (Papua New Guinea)

Papua New Guinea

Indonesia

Visit STRELLEY POOL, home of microscopic fossils from 3.4 billion years ago (Australia)

Christmas Island

Steer clear of the tiny but deadly IRUKANDJI JELLYFISH (Australi...

Australia

Survive in the outback with the DESERT GOBY (Australia)

Explore the mini village COCKINGTON GREEN GARDENS (Australia)

Take the plunge with the LITTLE PENGUIN (Australia)

Search for hiding garden gnomes at the ASHCOMBE MAZE (Australia)

Tasmania

Flinders Island

Hawaiian Islands

Federated States
of Micronesia

Marshall
Islands

South
Pacific
Ocean

Tuvalu

Solomon
Islands

New
Caledonia   Vanuatu

Marvel at the little lights
of the WAITOMO
GLOWWORM CAVES
(New Zealand)

Fiji   Samoa   French
Polynesia

Tonga

Visit Middle Earth
with a HOBBITON
MOVIE SET TOUR
(New Zealand)

New
Zealand

Hike the hills
and stop off at a
MINIATURE HUT
(New Zealand)

PAPUA NEW GUINEA

13

This little frog hides among dead leaves on the forest floor. The male's mating call sounds like that of an insect, making it very difficult to track down.

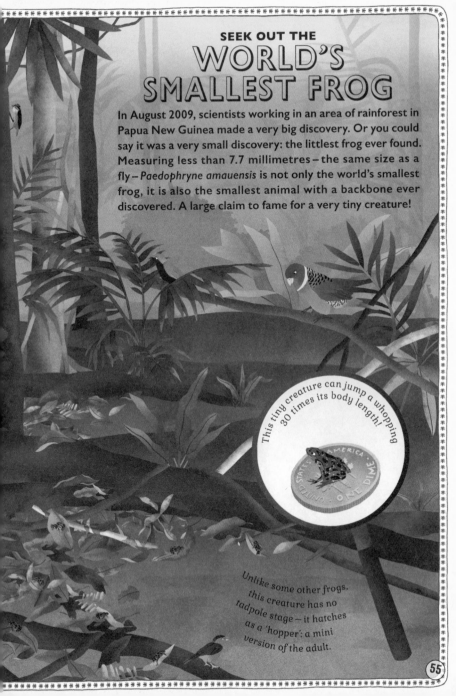

SEEK OUT THE
WORLD'S SMALLEST FROG

In August 2009, scientists working in an area of rainforest in Papua New Guinea made a very big discovery. Or you could say it was a very small discovery: the littlest frog ever found. Measuring less than 7.7 millimetres – the same size as a fly – *Paedophryne amauensis* is not only the world's smallest frog, it is also the smallest animal with a backbone ever discovered. A large claim to fame for a very tiny creature!

This tiny creature can jump a whopping 30 times its body length!

Unlike some other frogs, this creature has no tadpole stage – it hatches as a 'hopper': a mini version of the adult.

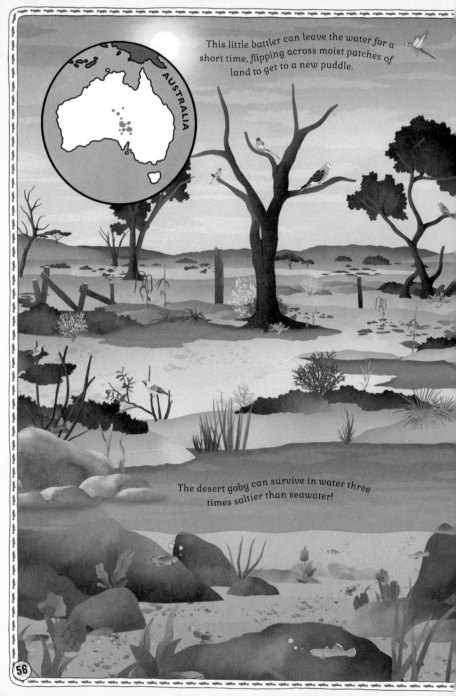

AUSTRALIA

This little battler can leave the water for a short time, flipping across moist patches of land to get to a new puddle.

The desert goby can survive in water three times saltier than seawater!

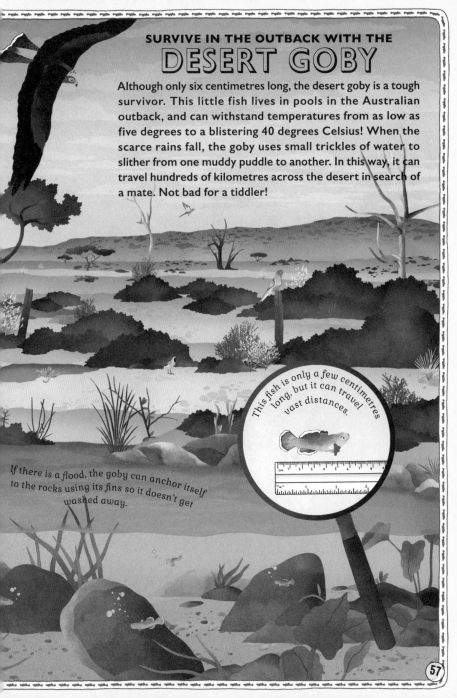

SURVIVE IN THE OUTBACK WITH THE
DESERT GOBY

Although only six centimetres long, the desert goby is a tough survivor. This little fish lives in pools in the Australian outback, and can withstand temperatures from as low as five degrees to a blistering 40 degrees Celsius! When the scarce rains fall, the goby uses small trickles of water to slither from one muddy puddle to another. In this way, it can travel hundreds of kilometres across the desert in search of a mate. Not bad for a tiddler!

This fish is only a few centimetres long, but it can travel vast distances.

If there is a flood, the goby can anchor itself to the rocks using its fins so it doesn't get washed away.

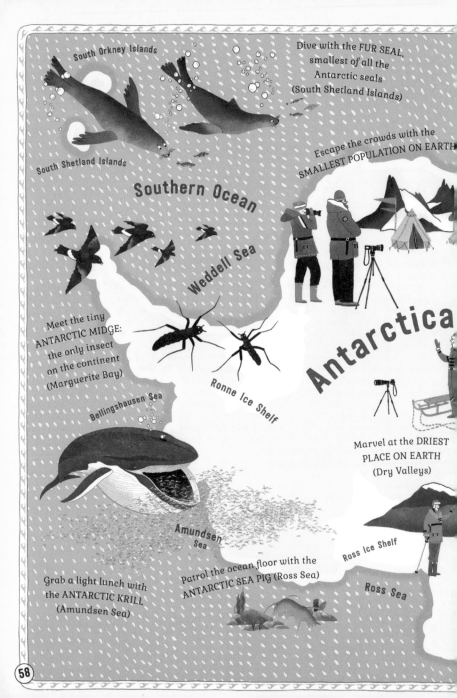

South Orkney Islands

Dive with the FUR SEAL, smallest of all the Antarctic seals (South Shetland Islands)

South Shetland Islands

Escape the crowds with the SMALLEST POPULATION ON EARTH

Southern Ocean

Weddell Sea

Meet the tiny ANTARCTIC MIDGE: the only insect on the continent (Marguerite Bay)

Antarctica

Ronne Ice Shelf

Bellingshausen Sea

Marvel at the DRIEST PLACE ON EARTH (Dry Valleys)

Amundsen Sea

Ross Ice Shelf

Grab a light lunch with the ANTARCTIC KRILL (Amundsen Sea)

Patrol the ocean floor with the ANTARCTIC SEA PIG (Ross Sea)

Ross Sea

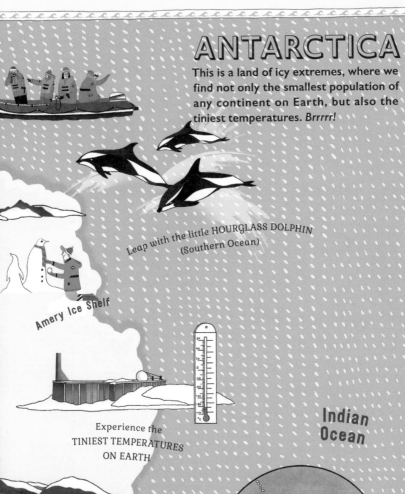

ANTARCTICA

This is a land of icy extremes, where we find not only the smallest population of any continent on Earth, but also the tiniest temperatures. *Brrrrr!*

Leap with the little HOURGLASS DOLPHIN
(Southern Ocean)

Amery Ice Shelf

Experience the
TINIEST TEMPERATURES
ON EARTH

Indian
Ocean

Tasman
Sea

Zoom in on the MOSS PIGLET –
a microscopic creature able to survive in
extreme conditions (Victoria Land)

59

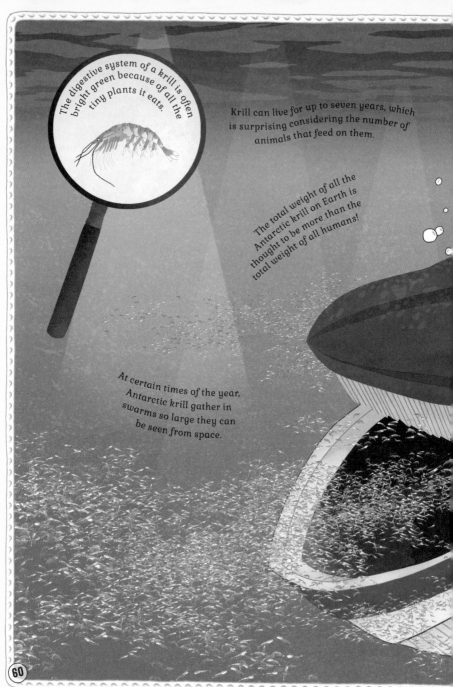

The digestive system of a krill is often bright green because of all the tiny plants it eats.

Krill can live for up to seven years, which is surprising considering the number of animals that feed on them.

The total weight of all the Antarctic krill on Earth is thought to be more than the total weight of all humans!

At certain times of the year, Antarctic krill gather in swarms so large they can be seen from space.

GRAB A LIGHT LUNCH WITH THE
ANTARCTIC KRILL

Small in size but huge in importance, Antarctic krill are the engine that powers the Antarctic food chain. These tiny, shrimp-like creatures measure only about five centimetres long, but they gather in enormous swarms, numbering millions. Most of the animals in the Antarctic – whales, seals, birds, and fish – depend on krill as a key part of their diet. Each day, a single blue whale can guzzle over 3.6 tonnes of krill – that's the same weight as an African elephant!

SOUTHERN OCEAN

CAN YOU FIND?

There are so many miniature things to spot throughout this book – not just
the bonsai trees or the fairy castle that first sent you on your adventures. See
if you can remember where you've spotted the items below, and go back to
these destinations to find them. What other things can you spot along the way?

Firefighters, **Bekonscot**

Windmill, **Madurodam**

Neon snail, **Berlin**

Stegosaurus, **Lyon**

Penguins, **Vienna**

Snake, **Madagascar**

Butterfly, **Namibia**

Signalman, **Northlandz**

Ferris wheel, **Northlandz**

Harp, **Fairy Castle**

Caterpillar, **South-west USA**

Sealing wax, **San Francisco**

Parakeet, **Dominican Republic**

Hummingbird nest, **Cuba**

Cascade bonsai, **Omiya**

Whale netsuke, **Kyoto**

Space teddy, **South Korea**

Six seahorses, **Indonesia**

Tiger parrot, **Papua New Guinea**

Budgerigar, **Australia**

Bourke's parrot, **Australia**

OTHER TITLES IN THE ATLAS OF ADVENTURES SERIES

First published in Great Britain in 2016 by Wide Eyed Editions,
an imprint of Aurum Press, 74–77 White Lion Street, London N1 9PF
QuartoKnows.com
Visit our blogs at QuartoKnows.com
Atlas of Animal Adventures copyright © Aurum Press Ltd 2016
Illustrations copyright © Lucy Letherland 2016

A catalogue record for this book is available from the British Library.

ISBN 978-1-84780-909-4
Illustrated with coloured inks

Set in Festivo, Gabriela and Gill Sans Shadow

Designed by Joe Hales and Andrew Watson
Published by Rachel Williams

Printed in China

1 3 5 7 9 8 6 4 2

MIX
Paper from
responsible sources
FSC® C104723
www.fsc.org